BRIGHT INTERVALS

Prayers for Paschal People

James Bitney

WINSTON PRESS

Unless otherwise indicated, all Scripture texts in this work are taken from *The New American Bible,* copyright © 1970 by the Confraternity of Christian Doctrine, Washington, D.C. Used by permission of the copyright owner. All rights reserved.
Scripture texts appearing on pages 74 and 30 are from *The Jerusalem Bible,* copyright © 1966 by Darton, Longman & Todd, Ltd., and Doubleday and Company, Inc. Used by permission of the publisher.

Photographs:
Cover — Robert Friedman
page two — Paul Conklin
page twelve — Vernon Sigl
page fifty-six — Roger Schaffhausen

Library of Congress Catalog Card Number: 81-70843
ISBN: 0-86683-669-1
Printed in the United States of America
5 4 3 2 1

Winston Press   430 Oak Grove   Minneapolis, Minnesota 55403

ACKNOWLEDGMENTS

I am full of gratitude to many: to Father Stephen Adrian and Father Richard Moudry for their vision and insights; to Richelle Koller for her enthusiasm and push; to Yvette Nelson, friend and poet, for her criticism and strong support; to my mother for the soul in these prayers; to my family for all the bright intervals they have given; and to the people of the church of Christ the King, who are truly paschal people.

To Susan,
the brightest of all

Be not forgetful of prayer. Every time you pray,
if your prayer is sincere, there will be a new
feeling and new meaning in it, which will give
you fresh courage.

FYODOR DOSTOEVSKY
The Brothers Karamazov[1]

CONTENTS

APPENDIX: USING BRIGHT INTERVALS WITH AND FOR CATECHUMENS

INTRODUCTION

The Paschal Mystery — Christ's life, death, and resurrection — marks and shapes our lives. The Paschal Mystery breaks into our lives in many ways, but especially in experiences of agony, ecstasy, transition, conversion, and their combinations — all *passage* experiences. Because they are risky, exceptional, and liminal moments of heightened awareness or consciousness, such experiences can easily lead us to God. In passage moments we are at our limits, and we naturally yearn for the transcendent. Our truest response to such experiences is a *paschal* response: to undergo them, to die and be reborn. And when we pray at such times, our prayer is truly paschal prayer.

Paschal prayer — whether individual or communal — is a response to God and to God's inbreaking, a prayer which helps us through life's transitional crises. The prayers in this book do not intervene in, solve, or attempt to explain away paschal crises. Rather, they simply seek to give voice to what God is doing in them and in our lives. For when we are able to discern and speak the meaning of God's activity in our lives, we can also celebrate that meaning with others. And in the exchange between the praying paschal person and the paschal community we call Church, renewal and new life happens.

1

THE PASCHAL JOURNEY

THE PASCHAL JOURNEY HOME

We shall not cease from exploration
and the end of all our exploring
will be to arrive where we started
and to know the place for the first time.
T.S. ELIOT, "Little Gidding"[2]

The paschal journey is an ongoing process involving all who call themselves Christian. Rooted in the Paschal Mystery of Christ and begun in baptism, the journey is one of continual dying and rising which leads to reunion with God and with one another. In other words, it is a journey home.

Christians, after all, are a pilgrim people, heirs to a long history of journeying with God. Today, just as in the past, God's people are a people on the march. Our journey is neither a safe nor a comfortable one. It makes many demands upon its travelers. Hazards, road blocks, and dangerous curves mark its way. Nevertheless, we Christians believe that God walks apace with us, helping us to abandon the pitfalls of selfishness while leading us home.

As Christians, our task is to embark on the paschal journey, to face its dangers and surprises, and to share it with others. The prayers of this section punctuate the journey's steps which help us discover, reshape, and resolve ingrained attitudes of selfishness. These prayers call us to restore forgotten or abandoned relationships.

3

They invite and encourage reconciliation. And they celebrate God's welcoming us home.

Perhaps G. K. Chesterton best explained the paschal journey's destination when he wrote in "The House of Christmas":

> To an open house in evening
> home shall men come
> to an older place than Eden,
> and a taller town than Rome.
> To the end of the way of the wandering star,
> to the things that cannot be and that are,
> to the place where God was homeless
> and all men are at home.[3]

An old saying claims that "home is where the heart is." On the paschal journey we can discover our own hearts; and at the end of that journey, arrive where we began and lay our hearts to rest, secure in the heart of God—home at last.

PRAYER FOR RESCUE

Blessed are you, Lord our God and God of our forebears.
    You are our rescue.
    You break the bonds of death,
    yet we continually test and resist you.
Reveal yourself to us, Lord,
    and keep us safe
    under the shadow
    of your sheltering wings.
O blessed are you, Lord our God,
    oasis in our desert,
    water from rock.
Flood your chosen ones with mercy.
    Cherish us
    beyond our wildest dreams.
Indeed, you are to be blest, Lord, our helper and guide.
    Lead us to the waters
    of eternal life.
May our faults be swept away
    by the torrent of your
    boundless compassion.
Hear this prayer offered in the name
    of the One who is flesh to your life-promise,
    the name that courses through us
    like a river in parched land,
Christ Jesus the Lord.
Amen.

PRAYER FOR ILLUMINATION OF HEART

Lord, you plumb the depths of the darkest soul.
You uncover hidden faults and cleanse all hearts
   in the light of your truth.
You gather a people and call them your own,
   not those who are saved,
   but those who know they stand
   in need of salvation.
Listen to this prayer for all
   in the circle of sinners and saints.
Lord, look with love on the hearts of your children
   and mark out the progress we make.
Put sinews in your revealing Word, O Lord,
   to strengthen us on our way.
Increase our faith.
Never let our failings crush us,
   but accept our repentance
   and grant us a portion of your unbounded mercy
   in Christ Jesus the Lord.
Amen.

PRAYER FOR VISION

Lord God, your all-seeing eye pierces to the heart
and illumines the dark night of the soul.
    Cast your bright eye
    on all you have chosen to call into light.
Lord God, you sent Jesus the Christ,
    the Author of Light,
    to strip away the scales from our eyes.
Help your chosen ones
    to abandon the old blindness
    and come to bask in his glorious rays.
Grant us also your guiding Spirit, Lord,
    to wipe clean the sin-streaked windows
    of our souls.
Expand our horizons, clear our vision,
    and lead us to the celebration
    of the Day of Great Light.
Lord, the way to new vision lies before us.
Bring us to union with you,
    with Christ, and the Spirit,
    a union to last forever and ever.
Amen.

PRAYER FOR ATONEMENT AND MERCY

Lord, you bring us the good news
    that you are a God who forgives!
Carry this good news
    to all who strive to celebrate
    your loving mercy.
Join us to yourself, Lord.
    Let us be at one with you.
Give us hearts of flesh,
    hearts big enough to welcome you
    into our lives.
May the revelation of your bountiful care
    fill us with peace.
And may this prayer made in faith
    draw us to you through
Christ Jesus, our merciful Lord.
Amen.

PRAYER FOR RECONCILIATION

Lord our God,
  you welcome us as wayward children.
You rejoice at our return
  like the finder of a long-lost coin.
For our sakes
  you have risked all,
  sold all,
  and purchased us at great price.
Your generosity overwhelms us.
Bless us who have sought you, O Lord.
Usher us into the hospitality prepared
  for those who love you,
  and welcome us home.
Bring all of us to see you eye to eye,
  face to face.
And remind us of your
  resplendent covenant,
Of your amazing promise
  that we *can* come home *again*
Through Christ Jesus, our Lord.
Amen.

PRAYER FOR NEW LIFE

May your name be glorified always,
  O Ruler of life and death!
Rain down your power and providence
  on all striving to answer
  your home-call.
Strengthen our commitment to follow without
    faltering
  and to serve without sin
  the One you have sent to lead all home to you,
Christ Jesus the Lord,
  death-defier,
  life-giver,
  today, tomorrow, and into eternity.
Amen.

PRAYER FOR THE PASCHAL JOURNEY

Lord God,
you call all of us to renewal,
to undertake the paschal journey
of dying and rebirth.
Your all-embracing mercy
summons our deepest thanks.
Guide us, O Lord,
and harken to our prayer.

Look upon your chosen ones,
and in times of darkness
turn our eyes to the bright day
of our journey's end.
The hour of your reign is dawning for us.
Attune us to your call
to pilgrimage.

Lead us onward, Lord,
in response to your gracious summons.
Form new hearts within us,
hearts restless until they rest in you.
Lead us to new life in the sign of renewal:
the triumphant cross.

We place this prayer before you
bound with Jesus' name.
In him may our journey continue;
through him may your name be blest
now and forever.
Amen.

THE PASCHAL SEASONS

CELEBRATING THE YEARLY CYCLE OF PRAYER

Why does the celebration of time and seasons of time rank so highly in the lives of Christians? First of all, our God is a God of time. We identify God in terms of time, not of space, and by real, historical events which take place in time. None of us can possess time. We can spend it or waste it and not really save it. We can conquer, possess, and even transcend things or space; but time conquers, possesses, and transcends us. God alone can possess time. In time we encounter God, and in time God encounters us. Thus, in our celebration of time we discover ourselves and eternity as well. Unfortunately, we do not always make this discovery easily. Therefore, as Christians we mark time in order to consecrate it, to get in touch with the God who orders not only all things but all time as well.

As Christians, we also celebrate time and seasons of time because of our deeply rooted human needs. Our seasonal celebrations give tangible and meaningful expression to a variety of human emotions and needs. Even though the Christian seasons developed as catechetical methods of expressing the diversity of God's presence in our lives, they developed also from the very core of our human need to discover the meaning of life, of life events, and of the dyings and risings of which life is composed. In different ways, then, every Christian season is deeply paschal. Each celebrates a particular expression or moment of Christ's Paschal Mystery—his dying and rising—for us. Each paschal season declares that God dwells in time, that Christians also live in time, and that all time is changed forever by the life, death, and resurrection of the Lord Jesus Christ.

Triduum

Fired by the paschal experience of the resurrection of the Lord, the early Christians began to perceive in a new way both time and the life contained in it. Their belief in, and experience of, the resurrection created a joy in the Christian community that expressed itself in the community's vision that God was abroad in their lives and history. The early Church celebrated this perception at the Table of the Lord on Sunday, the Lord's Day, and at its annual celebration of the great Sunday, Easter, the Christian "pasch." As time passed, the early Christians discovered that the richness of the Paschal Mystery demanded more than one celebration or festival day to plumb its depths. Therefore they expanded the celebration to a three-day festival called the *Triduum* (Good Friday, Holy Saturday, and Easter Sunday) in order to better incorporate into their lives the many aspects of that mystery.

Triduum is not merely a chronological account of the suffering, death, and resurrection of Jesus; Triduum is indivisible. Each day of Triduum portrays a different facet of the one great mystery of Jesus' death and resurrection. The three days help us realize that we too are an integral part of the Paschal Mystery. They celebrate the Christian passover from death to new life. All three days are death *and* resurrection; all three days are Easter.

The Season of Easter

The paschal experience of coming to new life was so powerful in the lives of Christians that it spawned its own season of celebration, the Season of Easter, whose joy extended fifty days. The early Christians called this entire period Pentecost (from the Greek word meaning *fifty*);

and they celebrated the fifty days as a single feast. The season terminated on the fiftieth day, also called Pentecost. Christians celebrated the fiftieth day as a commemoration of the ascension of the Lord and as the day of the outpouring of the Holy Spirit. Over the centuries, Christians gradually came to celebrate the resurrection, ascension, and the giving of the Holy Spirit on separate days. Nevertheless, this separation does not dissolve the unity of the season. From Triduum until the day of Pentecost, Christians celebrate one feast—the paschal feast of Easter.

The Season of Lent

Influenced by Triduum and the fifty-day celebration of Easter, which were highlighted by the ritual initiation and welcoming of new members into their fellowship, Christians eventually developed a season of preparation for that initiation.

The Christian community spent the days before Easter preparing candidates for admission to the faith community. This period culminated in the rituals of the Easter Vigil (Baptism, Confirmation, and Eucharist), which formally initiated the candidates into, and gave them a share in, the Paschal Mystery. Primarily, therefore, the content and mood of the preparation for Easter was initiatory.

As time passed and the Church began to recognize that some members of its already initiated community had strayed from the path Christ had set for them, the days prior to Easter also became a time for atonement. Christians who had sinned and fallen from baptismal grace undertook a discipline of penitence leading to change of heart. Before the celebration of the Easter Triduum, the Church reconciled these penitents to God and to the community. The lenten period of preparation took on a tone and atmosphere of reparation as well as of initiation.

Eventually the days of preparation for initiates and penitents came to define what we now know as the forty (actually, forty-four) days of Lent. Influenced by the conversion journey of these two groups, the entire Christian community developed practices by which it readied itself for Easter by renewing its own commitment to the paschal life which Easter, *the* paschal feast, demands. Thus Lent became a season of initiation, reparation, and restoration.

Throughout the centuries, the relative importance of these three components of Lent varied. Today all three remain wedded to the Lenten season. All three are important and necessary for our understanding and celebration not only of Lent and Easter but of the whole paschal life.

The Seasons of Advent and Christmas

The season of Advent, a period of preparation for Christmas, developed only after the early Christians had begun to celebrate the feast of Christmas. Sometime between the years A.D. 274 and 354 the Church chose to celebrate the nativity of the Lord on December twenty-fifth. The early Christians wanted to counter the celebration of the pagan feast *Sol Invictus,* the Unconquerable Sun, which the Roman emperor Aurelian inaugurated in the year A.D. 274 for the benefit of the Roman Legion. This pagan feast, set during the winter solstice, celebrated the gradual lengthening of daylight and the growing power of the sun.

In an anonymous Christian document dating from the late third or early fourth century, we read ". . . now they [pagans] call this day Birthday of the Unconquerable Sun! Who indeed is so unconquerable as our Lord, who overthrew and conquered death? And as for talking about the birthday of the Sun! He [Christ] is the Sun of Justice, He of whom the prophet Malachi said:

'For you who fear my name there will arise the Sun of Justice, with healing in his wings.'"

From their earliest celebration, therefore, Christmas and Advent were viewed as paschal seasons, seasons in which Christians celebrated Christ's coming among us to banish the fear of darkness, to overthrow death, and to lead us to light and new life. The season of Advent prepares us for just that sort of paschal coming. At the same time, Advent also prepares us for the coming of Christ at the end of all time. Like all other paschal seasons, the seasons of Advent and Christmas immerse us in the totality of the Paschal Mystery and celebrate our yearly living out of the paschal life.

This section of *Bright Intervals* is designed to help individuals, families, or larger groupings respond to the presence of the Paschal Lord who owns, marks, and shapes our time.

DAILY PRAYERS FOR ADVENT

The following services of daily prayer may be used by individuals, households, or prayer groups. Center these services around the Advent Wreath and candles, lighting the appropriate number of candles for each day of prayer (one candle for the first week of Advent, two candles for the second week, and so on). You will also need a supply of small candles. Plain white birthday candles will do nicely. At the conclusion of each prayer service, light one of the small candles and allow it to burn out completely. While this happens, do or say nothing. Simply watch and take the time to experience the light, the darkness, the quiet, and the waiting which is Advent.

Sundays of Advent

GATHERING

Leader: May the grace and peace of the King of Kings, Christ Jesus the Lord, be with us now and for endless days.

All: Until God's Kingdom dawns.

Leader: Fired by the Advent light and circled by this wreath of hope, we await the coming of our God. The Lord invites us on a journey from hostility to hospitality, a pilgrimage from darkness to light.

All: We await the advent of the Hope of Ages who comes to dwell as Guest-in-Our-Hearts and to draw all creation home to the Father.

Leader: Maranatha! Come, O Root of Jesse! You are the Tree of Life!

All: Forever may you be blest.

PRAYERS FOR INTERCESSION

Leader: As we wait for the coming of the Messiah, let us remember God's constant presence in our lives and set our prayers before the Lord.

(Invite everyone present to offer personal prayer or petition.)

PSALM

(Recite the Psalm together, or alternate the verses.)
Psalm 72
Antiphon: Bless the name of the Lord forever.
O God, with your judgment endow the king,
    and with your justice, the king's son;
He shall govern your people with justice
    and your afflicted ones with judgment.

The mountains shall yield peace for the people,
    and the hills justice.
He shall defend the afflicted among the people,
    save the children of the poor,
    and crush the oppressor.

May he endure as long as the sun,
    and like the moon through all generations.
He shall be like rain coming down on the meadow,
    like the showers watering the earth.
Justice shall flower in his days,
    and profound peace, till the moon be no more.

May he rule from sea to sea.
    and from the River to the ends of the earth.
His foes shall bow before him,
    and his enemies shall lick the dust.
The kings of Tarshish and the Isles shall offer gifts;
    the kings of Arabia and Seba shall bring tribute.
All kings shall pay him homage,
    all nations shall serve him.

For he shall rescue the poor man when he cries out,
and the afflicted when he has no one to help him.
He shall have pity for the lowly and the poor;
the lives of the poor he shall save.
From fraud and violence he shall redeem them,
and precious shall their blood be in his sight.

Blessed be the Lord, the God of Israel,
who alone does wondrous deeds.
And blessed forever be his glorious name;
may the whole earth be filled with his glory.
Amen. Amen.
Antiphon: Bless the name of the Lord forever.

CONCLUSION
Using one of the Advent candles, light the small birth-day candle, and then extinguish the Advent candle(s). Allow the small candle to burn out completely. Say nothing during this time; simply allow yourself to watch and wait.

Mondays of Advent

GATHERING
Leader: May the grace and peace of the Promised One, Christ Jesus the Lord, be with us now and for endless days.

All: Until God's Kingdom dawns.

Leader: Fired by the Advent light and circled by this wreath of hope, we await the coming of our God. The Lord invites us on a journey from hostility to hospitality, a pilgrimage from darkness to light.

All: We await the advent of the Prince of Peace who comes to dwell as Guest-in-Our-Hearts and to draw all creation home to the Father.

Leader: Maranatha! Come, O Adonai! You are the Gate to the City of God.

All: Forever may you be blest.

PRAYERS OF INTERCESSION
Leader: As we wait for the coming of the Messiah, let us
remember God's constant presence in our lives
and set our prayers before the Lord.
(Invite everyone present to offer personal prayer or
petition.)

PSALM
(Recite the Psalm together, or alternate the verses.)
Psalm 126
Antiphon: The Lord has done great things for us.
When the Lord brought back the captives of Zion,
we were like men dreaming.
Then our mouth was filled with laughter,
and our tongue with rejoicing.
Then they said among the nations,
"The Lord has done great things for them."
The Lord has done great things for us;
we are glad indeed.

Restore our fortunes, O Lord,
like the torrents in the southern desert.
Those that sow in tears
shall reap rejoicing.
Although they go forth weeping.
carrying the seed to be sown,
They shall come back rejoicing,
carrying their sheaves.
Antiphon: The Lord has done great things for us.

CONCLUSION
Using one of the Advent candles, light the small birthday candle and then extinguish the Advent candle(s).
Allow the small candle to burn out completely. Say
nothing during this time; simply allow yourself to watch
and wait.

Tuesdays of Advent

GATHERING

Leader: May the grace and peace of the living Word of God, Christ Jesus the Lord, be with us now and for endless days.

All: Until God's Kingdom dawns.

Leader: Fired by the Advent light and circled by this wreath of hope, we await the coming of our God. The Lord invites us on a journey from hostility to hospitality, a pilgrimage from darkness to light.

All: We await the advent of the Word Made Flesh who comes to dwell as Guest-in-Our-Hearts and to draw all creation home to the Father.

Leader: Maranatha! Come, O Bright Morning Star! You are the Dayspring from on high.

All: Forever may you be blest.

PRAYERS OF INTERCESSION

Leader: As we wait for the coming of the Messiah, let us remember God's constant presence in our lives and set our prayers before the Lord.

(Invite everyone present to offer personal prayer or petition.)

PSALM

(Recite the Psalm together, or alternate the verses.)

Psalm 122

Antiphon: We approach God's house with shouts of joy!

I rejoiced because they said to me,
    "We will go up to the house of the Lord."
And now we have set foot
    within your gates, O Jerusalem—
Jerusalem built as a city
    with compact unity.

To it the tribes go up,
  the tribes of the Lord,
According to the decree for Israel,
  to give thanks to the name of the Lord.
In it are set up judgment seats,
  seats for the house of David.

Pray for the peace of Jerusalem!
  May those who love you prosper!
May peace be within your walls,
  prosperity in your buildings.
Because of my relatives and friends
  I will say, "Peace be within you!"
Because of the house of the Lord, our God,
  I will pray for your good.
Antiphon: We approach God's house with shouts of joy!

CONCLUSION
Using one of the Advent candles, light the small birthday candle and then extinguish the Advent candle(s).
Allow the small candle to burn out completely. Say
nothing during this time; simply allow yourself to watch
and wait.

Wednesdays of Advent

GATHERING
Leader: May the grace and peace of the Wisdom of
        God, Christ Jesus the Lord, be with us now and
        for endless days.
   All: Until God's Kingdom dawns.
Leader: Fired by the Advent light and circled by this
        wreath of hope, we await the coming of our
        God. The Lord invites us on a journey from
        hostility to hospitality, a pilgrimage from
        darkness to light.
   All: We await the advent of the Shepherd of Israel
        who comes to dwell as Guest-in-Our-Hearts
        and to draw all creation home to the Father.

Leader: Maranatha! Come, O gracious Giver-of-Knowledge! You lead us all to the Truth.

All: Forever may you be blest.

PRAYERS OF INTERCESSION

Leader: As we wait for the coming of the Messiah, let us remember God's constant presence in our lives and set our prayers before the Lord.

(Invite everyone present to offer personal prayer or petition.)

PSALM

(Recite the Psalm together, or alternate the verses.)

Psalm 80

Antiphon: Restore us, O Lord of hosts.

O shepherd of Israel, hearken,
    O guide of the flock of Joseph!
From your throne upon the cherubim, shine forth
    before Ephraim, Benjamin and Manasseh.
Rouse your power,
    and come to save us.
        O Lord of hosts, restore us;
            if your face shine upon us,
                then we shall be safe.

O Lord of hosts, how long will you burn with anger
    while your people pray?
You have fed them with the bread of tears
    and given them tears to drink in ample measure.
You have left us to be fought over by our neighbors,
    and our enemies mock us.
        O Lord of hosts, restore us;
            if your face shine upon us,
                then we shall be safe.
Antiphon: Restore us, O Lord of hosts.

CONCLUSION

Using one of the Advent candles, light the small birthday candle and then extinguish the Advent candle(s). Allow the small candle to burn out completely. Say nothing during this time; simply allow yourself to watch and wait.

Thursdays of Advent

GATHERING

Leader: May the grace and peace of the Wonder-Counselor, Christ Jesus the Lord, be with us now and for endless days.

All: Until God's Kingdom dawns.

Leader: Fired by the Advent light and circled by this wreath of hope, we await the coming of our God. The Lord invites us on a journey from hostility to hospitality, a pilgrimage from darkness to light.

All: We await the advent of the God-Hero who comes to dwell as Guest-in-Our-Hearts and to draw all creation home to the Father.

Leader: Maranatha! Come, O God-Always-With-Us! You are flesh of our flesh and bone of our bone.

All: Forever may you be blest.

PRAYERS OF INTERCESSION

Leader: As we wait for the coming of the Messiah, let us remember God's constant presence in our lives and set our prayers before the Lord.

(Invite everyone present to offer personal prayer or petition.)

PSALM

(Recite the Psalm together, or alternate the verses.)

Psalm 146

Antiphon: I will praise the Lord all my days.

Praise the Lord, O my soul;
    I will praise the Lord all my life;
    I will sing praise to my God while I live.

Happy he whose help is the God of Jacob,
    whose hope is in the Lord, his God,
Who made heaven and earth,
    the sea and all that is in them;
Who keeps faith forever,
    secures justice for the oppressed,
    gives food to the hungry.
The Lord sets captives free;
    the Lord gives sight to the blind.
The Lord raises up those that were bowed down;
    the Lord loves the just.
The Lord protects strangers;
    the fatherless and the widow he sustains.
    but the way of the wicked he thwarts.
The Lord shall reign forever;
    your God, O Zion, through all generations.
Antiphon: I will praise the Lord all my days.

CONCLUSION

Using one of the Advent candles, light the small birth-day candle and then extinguish the Advent candle(s). Allow the small candle to burn out completely. Say nothing during this time; simply allow yourself to watch and wait.

Fridays of Advent

GATHERING

Leader: May the grace and peace of the Light of Life, Christ Jesus the Lord, be with us now and for endless days.

All: Until God's Kingdom dawns.

Leader: Fired by the Advent light and circled by this wreath of hope, we await the coming of our God. The Lord invites us on a journey from hostility to hospitality, a pilgrimage from darkness to light.

All: We await the advent of the King of Creation who comes to dwell as Guest-in-Our-Hearts and to draw all creation home to the Father.

Leader: Maranatha! Come, O Sun of Justice! You are the Lord of Love.

All: Forever may you be blessed.

PRAYERS OF INTERCESSION

Leader: As we wait for the coming of the Messiah, let us remember God's constant presence in our lives and set our prayers before the Lord.

(Invite everyone present to offer personal prayer or petition.)

PSALM

(Recite the Psalm together, or alternate the verses.)

Psalm 85

Antiphon: The Lord God will redeem us.

I will hear what God proclaims;
    the Lord—for he proclaims peace
To his people, and to his faithful ones,
    and to those who put in him their hope.
Near indeed is his salvation to those who fear him,
    glory dwelling in our land.
Kindness and truth shall meet;
    justice and peace shall kiss.
Truth shall spring out of the earth,
    and justice shall look down from heaven.

The Lord himself will give his benefits;
  our land shall yield its increase.
Justice shall walk before him,
  and salvation, along the way of his steps.
Antiphon: The Lord God will redeem us.

CONCLUSION
Using one of the Advent candles, light the small birthday candle and then extinguish the Advent candle(s). Allow the small candle to burn out completely. Say nothing during this time; simply allow yourself to watch and wait.

Saturdays of Advent

GATHERING
Leader: May the grace and peace of Emmanuel, Christ Jesus the Lord, be with us now and for endless days.

All: Until God's Kingdom dawns.

Leader: Fired by the Advent light and circled by this wreath of hope, we await the coming of our God. The Lord invites us on a journey from hostility to hospitality, a pilgrimage from darkness to light.

All: We await the advent of God-With-Us who comes to dwell as Guest-in-Our-Hearts and to draw all creation home to the Father.

Leader: Maranatha! Come, O Key of David! You are the unlocker of hearts, God's own Son.

All: Forever may you be blessed.

PRAYERS OF INTERCESSION
Leader: As we wait for the coming of the Messiah, let us remember God's constant presence in our lives and set our prayers before the Lord.

(Invite everyone present to offer personal prayer or petition.)

PSALM
(Recite the Psalm together, or alternate the verses.)
Psalm 89
Antiphon: I will sing of God's love forever.
The favors of the Lord I will sing forever;
    through all generations my mouth
        shall proclaim your faithfulness.
For you have said, "My kindness is established
        forever";
    in heaven you have confirmed your faithfulness:
"I have made a covenant with my chosen one,
    I have sworn to David my servant:
Forever will I confirm your posterity
    and establish your throne for all generations."

Happy the people who know the joyful shout;
    in the light of your countenance, O Lord, they walk.
At your name they rejoice all the day,
    and through your justice they are exalted.
For you are the splendor of their strength,
    and by your favor our horn is exalted.
For to the Lord belongs our shield,
    and to the Holy One of Israel, our king.
Antiphon: I will sing of God's love forever.

CONCLUSION
Using one of the Advent candles, light the small birthday candle and then extinguish the Advent candle(s).
Allow the small candle to burn out completely. Say
nothing during this time; simply allow yourself to watch
and wait.

THE FEAST OF CHRISTMAS

When peaceful silence lay over all,
and night had run the half of her swift course,
down from the heavens, from the royal throne,
leaped your all-powerful Word;
into the heart of a doomed land the stern warrior leaped.
WISDOM 18:14-15,
The Jerusalem Bible

Praise be to you, O Lord,
for you have sent the Light of the World
to a people lost in darkness.
Your eternal Word has taken blood
and bone and flesh,
and deigned to call us
sisters and brothers.
There are no thanks sufficient
for such a gift.
All we can do is open our hearts
to that holy Word,
the Word you speak
with such chilling ferocity,
such dazzling beauty,
such comforting gentleness
in Emmanuel, who is Jesus the Christ.
May the fire of that Word melt
any hostility we still harbor,
any icy bitterness we have within us.
Then, with Emmanuel, we can say,
"All is calm, all is bright,"
for your Word is
God-with-Us
incarnating in us
now and forever.
Amen.

THE FEAST OF EPIPHANY

Lord,
on the feast of Jesus' manifestation
—as the festive story of Christmas draws to a close—
we find ourselves filled with memories,
joy and thanksgiving.
It is our faith
that the Lord of Light
will keep the warmth of this season
blazing within us, so that throughout winter days
we may continue to be
a people of warmth,
a people of hospitality,
a people of joy to the world,
truly a people who live and breathe
the story of Emmanuel.
Indeed, the Light of Christ has come into the world!
The Sun of Justice has dawned upon us!
The Promise of Ages has been fulfilled in us!
The Root of Jesse has blossomed in our midst!
The glory of the Lord shines 'round about us,
        and we are at peace.
Amen.

DAILY PRAYERS FOR LENT

Each of the following daily services of prayer may be held alone or in a group. Each begins with a greeting and an opening prayer. Scripture references are provided for the daily reading, five for each day of the week, corresponding to the five weeks of Lent. The service concludes with a blessing. Set a comfortable time each day to pray these prayers together. Focus the prayer around the symbol of Lent: a simple, bare cross.

Sundays of Lent

GREETING (Kneel)

Leader: In the name of the Lord who calls us to renewal, in the name of the God we seek, in the name of the Father, and of the Son, and of the Holy Spirit.

All: Amen.

Leader: May the life that flows from the cross of Christ fill our hearts and homes this holy season.

All: May it be so for us, and for all God's people.

OPENING PRAYER (Kneel)

Leader: Let us gather together in prayer.

All: Lord, you are our beginning and our end. You give us this gift of sacred time, this day of rest in you. Locked in your love, may we always hold fast to the promise of eternal sabbath with you and with your Son and Spirit, for ever and ever. Amen.

Leader: Let us set our thoughts on the compassionate Word of the Lord.

GOD'S WORD (Sit)

First Sunday: Romans 5:12-19 (The New Adam)

Second Sunday: 2 Timothy 1:8-11 (The God to whom you witness)

Third Sunday: Exodus 17:3-7 (Water from the rock)

Fourth Sunday: Mark 6:8-13 (Instruction on the apostolate)

Fifth Sunday: John 6:1-15 (Jesus feeding the multitudes)

(Pause for a few moments of prayerful reflection.)

CONCLUDING BLESSING (Stand. Join hands or place hands on one another's shoulders.)

Leader: May the divine Word dwell with us this day as we call upon its Author in blessing.

All: May the Lord, the Holy One, rescue us, give us new hearts, and bless us with the sign of the life-giving cross, the Father, and the Son, and the Holy Spirit. Amen.

Mondays of Lent

GREETING (Kneel)

Leader: In the name of the Lord who calls us to renewal, in the name of the God we seek, in the name of the Father, and of the Son, and of the Holy Spirit.

All: Amen.

Leader: May the life that flows from the cross of Christ fill our hearts and homes this holy season.

All: May it be so for us, and for all God's people.

OPENING PRAYER (Kneel)

Leader: Let us gather together in prayer.

All: Lord, we seek your face. We search you out to return to you with all our hearts. May your peace be ours in abundance and remain with us now and forever. Amen.

Leader: Let us set our thoughts on the compassionate Word of the Lord.

GOD'S WORD (Sit)

First Monday: Philippians 3:17-21 (Follow the cross of Christ)

Second Monday: 1 Thessalonians 5:14-23 (Prepare for Christ)

Third Monday; Romans 5:1-2, 5-8 (God's love is poured into our hearts)

Fourth Monday: Daniel 3:25, 34-43 (Receive us with contrite hearts)

Fifth Monday: Genesis 17:3-9 (God is the father of nations)

(Pause for a few moments of prayerful reflection.)

CONCLUDING BLESSING (Stand. Join hands or place hands on one another's shoulders.)

Leader: May the divine Word dwell with us this day as we call upon its Author in blessing.

All: May the Lord, the Holy One, rescue us, give us new hearts, and bless us with the sign of the life-giving cross, the Father, and the Son, and the Holy Spirit. Amen.

Tuesdays of Lent

GREETING (Kneel)

Leader: In the name of the Lord who calls us to renewal, in the name of the God we seek, in the name of the Father, and of the Son, and of the Holy Spirit.

All: Amen.

Leader: May the life that flows from the cross of Christ fill our hearts and homes this holy season.

All: May it be so for us, and for all God's people.

OPENING PRAYER (Kneel)

Leader: Let us gather together in prayer.

All: Our hearts prompt us to seek you, O Lord. We long for your countenance; hide not from us. May we hear your home-call and respond. And may your glory shine 'round about us now and forever. Amen.

Leader: Let us set our thoughts on the compassionate Word of the Lord.

GOD'S WORD (Sit)
First Tuesday: Ezekiel 18:20-28 (Look to a new life)
Second Tuesday: Matthew 23:1-12 (To whom are we likened?)
Third Tuesday: Luke 4:24-30 (Christ was sent for all)
Fourth Tuesday: Ezekiel 37:21-28 (I will make you into one people)
Fifth Tuesday: Isaiah 65:17-21 (A new heaven and a new earth)
(Pause for a few moments of prayerful reflection.)

CONCLUDING BLESSING (Stand. Join hands or place hands on one another's shoulders.)
Leader: May the divine Word dwell with us this day as we call upon its Author in blessing.
All: May the Lord, the Holy One, rescue us, give us new hearts, and bless us with the sign of the life-giving cross, the Father, and the Son, and the Holy Spirit. Amen.

Wednesdays of Lent

GREETING (Kneel)
Leader: In the name of the Lord who calls us to renewal, in the name of the God we seek, in the name of the Father, and of the Son, and of the Holy Spirit.
All: Amen.
Leader: May the life that flows from the cross of Christ fill our hearts and homes this holy season.
All: May it be so for us, and for all God's people.

OPENING PRAYER (Kneel)
Leader: Let us gather together in prayer.

All: O Lord, you are our rock; our foundation is secure. O Lord, you are our rescue; you give us wings! May our eyes be fixed on you always. And may you continue to pour your love into our hearts forever and ever. Amen.

Leader: Let us set our thoughts on the compassionate Word of the Lord.

GOD'S WORD (Sit)

First Wednesday: Mark 4:35-40 (Jesus calms a tempest)

Second Wednesday: Isaiah 49:8-15 (God's love for us)

Third Wednesday: Jeremiah 7:23-28 (I will be your God; You will be my people)

Fourth Wednesday: Mark 12:28-34 (The Lord our God is one)

Fifth Wednesday: Galatians 4:1-20 (A Christian is free)

(Pause for a few moments of prayerful reflection.)

CONCLUDING BLESSING (Stand. Join hands or place hands on one another's shoulders.)

Leader: May the divine Word dwell with us this day as we call upon its Author in blessing.

All: May the Lord, the Holy One, rescue us, give us new hearts, and bless us with the sign of the life-giving cross, the Father, and the Son, and the Holy Spirit. Amen.

Thursdays of Lent

GREETING (Kneel)

Leader: In the name of the Lord who calls us to renewal, in the name of the God we seek, in the name of the Father, and of the Son, and of the Holy Spirit.

All: Amen.

Leader: May the life that flows from the cross of Christ fill our hearts and homes this holy season.

All: May it be so for us, and for all God's people.

OPENING PRAYER (Kneel)

Leader: Let us gather together in prayer.

All: Lord, we are humble vessels, yet you fill us with your glorious presence. You gather us from the cobwebbed corners of the earth and polish us to a glow! Place a new spirit within us, Lord, that we may reflect the brilliance of your light now and forever. Amen.

Leader: Let us set our thoughts on the compassionate Word of the Lord.

GOD'S WORD (Sit)

First Thursday: Hosea 6:1-6 (Love, not sacrifice)

Second Thursday: Ephesians 5:8-14 (Light and darkness)

Third Thursday: John 5:1-3, 5-16 (Jesus cures)

Fourth Thursday: Wisdom 2:1, 12-22 (The Suffering Servant)

Fifth Thursday: Matthew 15:1-20 (We are more than the Pharisees)

(Pause for a few moments of prayerful reflection.)

CONCLUDING BLESSING (Stand. Join hands or place hands on one another's shoulders.)

Leader: May the divine Word dwell with us this day as we call upon its Author in blessing.

All: May the Lord, the Holy one, rescue us, give us new hearts, and bless us with the sign of the life-giving cross, the Father, and the Son, and the Holy Spirit. Amen.

Fridays of Lent

GREETING (Kneel)

Leader: In the name of the Lord who calls us to renewal, in the name of the God we seek, in the name of the Father, and of the Son, and of the Holy Spirit.

All: Amen.

Leader: May the life that flows from the cross of Christ fill our hearts and homes this holy season.
All: May it be so for us, and for all God's people.

OPENING PRAYER (Kneel)
Leader: Let us gather together in prayer.
All: Lord, you shower us with justice. You rescue us from death. You are our refuge, our touchstone in a tumultuous world. May we cleave to you with all our hearts so that your promise of resurrection might be ours, now and forever. Amen.
Leader: Let us set our thoughts on the compassionate Word of the Lord.

GOD'S WORD (Sit)
First Friday: Luke 18:31-34 (Prediction of the Passion)
Second Friday: Hebrews 13:1-21 (How to act)
Third Friday: Jeremiah 11:18-20 (The Lamb led to slaughter)
Fourth Friday: John 8:21-30 (I will be lifted up)
Fifth Friday: Ezekiel 37:12-14 (Resurrection through the Spirit)
(Pause for a few moments of prayerful reflection.)

CONCLUDING BLESSING (Stand. Join hands or place hands on one another's shoulders.)
Leader: May the divine Word dwell with us this day as we call upon its Author in blessing.
All: May the Lord, the Holy One, rescue us, give us new hearts, and bless us with the sign of the life-giving cross, the Father, and the Son, and the Holy Spirit. Amen.

Saturdays of Lent

GREETING (Kneel)
Leader: In the name of the Lord who calls us to renewal, in the name of the God we seek, in the name of

the Father, and of the Son, and of the Holy
Spirit.

All: Amen.

Leader: May the life that flows from the cross of Christ
fill our hearts and homes this holy season.

All: May it be so for us, and for all God's people.

OPENING PRAYER (Kneel)

Leader: Let us gather together in prayer.

All: Lord, we are overwhelmed that you have chosen
us and called us to life in you. Continue to show
us your kindness, that we might not fear to lay
aside our sinfulness and inhumanity, to
shoulder our cross and to follow you now and
forever. Amen.

Leader: Let us set our thoughts on the compassionate
Word of the Lord.

GOD'S WORD (Sit)

First Saturday: Isaiah 58:1-9 (True fasting)

Second Saturday: Ezekiel 34:11-16 (The Good
Shepherd)

Third Saturday: Joel 2:12-19 (Peace from the heart)

Fourth Saturday: Mark 14:17-25 (The Last Supper
discourse)

Fifth Saturday: Mark 2:18-22 (How shall we fast?)

(Pause for a few moments of prayerful reflection.)

CONCLUDING BLESSING (Stand. Join hands or place
hands on one another's shoulders.)

Leader: May the divine Word dwell with us this day as
we call upon its Author in blessing.

All: May the Lord, the Holy One, rescue us, give us
new hearts, and bless us with the sign of the
life-giving cross, the Father, and the Son, and
the Holy Spirit. Amen.

PRAYERS FOR THE TRIDUUM

Good Friday

Day of paradox,
day of darkness and light,
of evil and justice,
of death and rebirth!
On this day, Lord,
you remember us and restore us to life,
not by some sleight of hand
or conjurer's trick,
but by blood, nails, and wood—
rough-hewn sign of your new mandatum.
Under this sign we make our vigil,
knowing that you will never forget us
but will grant us a share
in the passion and compassion
of Christ.
Remember us, Lord,
in our own crucifixions,
in the abandonments and desolations
that cross our lives
and move us toward death.
Move us to resurrection, Lord.
Write our names large
in the Book of Life.
Shadow our living with the sign of the cross,
our dyings with your brilliant wings;
and sear into our memories forever
the meaning of this holy day
   not for what it was,
   but for what it promises
a day to call "good"
for all of our days.
Amen.

The Vigil of Easter

O holy night,
how can we sing your praises?
How can we hymn your charms?
You are the night of our longing
and the dawn of our future.
You are the mother of nights.

O night of fire,
blazing to light!
You banish all darkness.
You cast your bright beams
on the quick and the dead.

O night of good news!
Beginnings and middles
you now bring to their climax
as you speak out so clearly
the Word of the Lord.

O night of rebirth,
your water surges and refreshes
and pries our lives
from the fingers of death.

O night of the Spirit,
you glisten us with your unction
and overflow us with kingship
as you breathe your sweet breath
into our hearts.

O night of the banquet,
you heap us with blessing:
the bread more than bread,
tasting of welcome and life;
the cup more than wine,
the vintage of eons,
tasting of faith and slaking all thirsts.

O night of our Alpha
and night of Omega,
you transform a cross-shaped nation
into a people of resurrection,
a people reveling in Christ Jesus
here in our midst,
the Alleluia of our days
past, present, and into infinity.

O night,
there is none beside you,
inexpressible, inexplicable.
O night!
O holy night!
O night divine!
Amen.

Easter Sunday

This is the day the Lord has made.
Let us rejoice and be glad!

Blessed are you, Lord our God,
you who give us this remarkable day.
Because of this day we can
    break through the prisons of faults,
    step off the treadmills of fear,
    crack open even hearts of stone,
    and rise above our own selves.
For the Lord is risen!
Alleluia!

This is the day the Lord has made.
Let us rejoice and be glad!

Blessed are you, Lord our God,
you who give us this remarkable day.
This day has become the hub of life
around which all else revolves.
This day exiles time,

tips the world on its axis,
and reveals eternity's glory
like a peacock spreading its fan.
For the Lord is risen!
Alleluia!

This is the day the Lord has made.
Let us rejoice and be glad!

Blessed are you, Lord our God,
you who give us this remarkable day.
This day transforms the tree of destruction
into the life-giving tree:
   surprising in its flowering,
   its blossom is Christ,
   whose fragrance gives us life,
   whose blooming sets us free.
For the Lord is risen!
The Lord is risen indeed!
Alleluia!

DAILY PRAYERS FOR THE SEASON OF EASTER

The following prayer services—one for each day of the week—may be used in the home to help you celebrate the fifty-day season of Easter. The prayers for these days do not attempt to explain the meaning of the Easter festival. Rather, they reflect the difference Easter makes in our lives. Our Easter prayer is one way we "speak" and share with others our experience of the Paschal Mystery, our individual and communal dying and rising with Christ.

If you used the cross as a symbol to help you in your Lenten prayer, continue to use it during the Easter season. Decorate the cross with spring flowers, and add a white Easter candle and a bowl of water. As much as the words of prayer, our posture at prayer expresses our attitudes toward God and toward those with whom we pray. Thus, when praying these prayers, do so standing, for standing is a symbol of Easter. In fact, the word "resurrection" finds its roots in the Greek word, "anastasis," which means "standing up." When we pray standing, we proclaim with our bodies that we are a people of resurrection.

Sundays of Easter Season

BEGINNING
(All stand. The Leader lights the Easter candle.)
Leader: Christ is our light!
    All: Thanks be to God.
Leader: Let us rejoice in the living Lord.
    All: Alleluia! Amen.
Leader: May the new life won by our gracious Lord on this the first of days fill us with joy.
    All: May it be so for us and for all Easter people.

GATHERING

Leader: Let us call upon the God of life. (Pause a moment for silent prayer.)

Father of mercy, we no longer search for your Son among the dead. Christ is risen! He has become the Lord of life! From the waters of death you raise us with him, and you quicken our hearts with the fire of your Holy Spirit. Increase the love we share, strengthen our faith, and help us grow into the fullness of life with you through Christ Jesus our Lord.

All: Amen.

PSALM OF REJOICING

(All recite together, or alternate the verses.)

Psalm 118

Alleluia, Alleluia.

I will give thanks to you, for you have answered me
   and have been my savior.

The stone which the builders rejected
   has become the cornerstone.
By the Lord has this been done;
   it is wonderful in our eyes.

This is the day the Lord has made;
   let us be glad and rejoice in it.
O Lord, grant salvation!
   O Lord, grant prosperity!
Blessed is he who comes in the name of the Lord;
   we bless you from the house of the Lord.
The Lord is God, and he has given us light.
Join in procession with leafy boughs
   up to the horns of the altar.
You are my God, and I give thanks to you;
   O my God, I extol you.
Give thanks to the Lord, for he is good;
   for his kindness endures forever.
Alleluia, Alleluia.

CONCLUSION

(The leader takes the bowl of water to each person in the group. Each person marks his or her forehead with water in the sign of the cross saying:)
Christ has died,
Christ is risen,
Christ will come again.
Alleluia!
(If you wish, conclude with an Easter song everyone knows.)

Mondays of Easter Season

BEGINNING

(All stand. The Leader lights the Easter candle.)
Leader: Christ is our light!
    All: Thanks be to God.
Leader: Let us rejoice in the King of the universe, exult in the God of life.
    All: Alleluia! Amen.
Leader: May the joy of the new life won by Christ fill all our days.
    All: May it be so for us and for all Easter people.

GATHERING

Leader: Let us call upon the God of life. (Pause a moment for silent prayer.)
Gracious Father, author of all words of truth, a people once awash in darkness have listened to your Word and followed your Son as he destroyed the gates of death. Hear the prayer of this newborn people and strengthen us to answer your call. May we rise and come forth into the light of day to stand in your presence until eternity dawns. This we ask through Christ Jesus our Lord.
    All: Amen.

PSALM OF REJOICING
(All recite together, or alternate the verses.)
Psalm 150
Alleluia, Alleluia.
Praise the Lord in his sanctuary,
  praise him in the firmament of his strength.
Praise him for his mighty deeds,
  praise him for his sovereign majesty.
Praise him with the blast of the trumpet,
  praise him with lyre and harp,
Praise him with timbrel and dance,
  praise him with strings and pipe.
Praise him with sounding cymbals.
  praise him with clanging cymbals.
Let everything that has breath praise the Lord!
Alleluia, Alleluia.

CONCLUSION
(The leader takes the bowl of water to each person in the
group. Each person marks his or her forehead with water
in the sign of the cross saying:)
Christ has died,
Christ is risen,
Christ will come again.
Alleluia!
(If you wish, conclude with an Easter song everyone
knows.)

Tuesdays of Easter Season

BEGINNING
(All stand. The leader lights the Easter candle.)
Leader: Christ is our light!
  All: Thanks be to God.
Leader: Let us rejoice in the Shepherd of Israel, our
      Savior and Lord.
  All: Alleluia! Amen.

Leader: May the salvation won for us by the blood of the Lamb lead us to peace.
All: May it be so for us and for all Easter people.

GATHERING

Leader: Let us call upon the God of life. (Pause a moment for silent prayer.) Father, although your people may walk in the valley of darkness, they fear no evil, for they follow in faith the call of the Shepherd whom you have sent for their hope and strength. Attune our minds to the sound of his voice and lead our steps in the path he has shown, that we may know the strength of his outstretched arm and enjoy the light of your presence forever.
All: Amen.

PSALM OF REJOICING

(All recite together, or alternate the verses.)
Psalm 98
Alleluia, Alleluia.
Sing to the Lord a new song,
    for he has done wondrous deeds;
His right hand has won victory for him,
    his holy arm.

The Lord has made his salvation known:
    in the sight of the nations he has revealed his
        justice.
He has remembered his kindness and his faithfulness
    toward the house of Israel.
All the ends of the earth have seen
    the salvation by our God.

Sing joyfully to the Lord, all you lands;
    break into song; sing praise.
Sing praise to the Lord with the harp,
    with the harp and melodious song.

With trumpets and the sound of the horn
  sing joyfully before the King, the Lord.
Alleluia, Alleluia.

CONCLUSION
(The leader takes the bowl of water to each person in the group. Each person marks his or her forehead with water in the sign of the cross saying:)
Christ has died,
Christ is risen,
Christ will come again.
Alleluia!
(If you wish, conclude with an Easter song everyone knows.)

Wednesdays of Easter Season

BEGINNING
(All stand. The Leader lights the Easter candle.)
Leader: Christ is our light!
  All: Thanks be to God.
Leader: Let us rejoice in Christ, the harrower of death.
  All: Alleluia! Amen.
Leader: May the way Christ paved for us lead us to the fullness of life.
  All: May it be so for us and for all Easter people.

GATHERING
Leader: Let us call upon the God of life. (Pause a moment for silent prayer.)
  Father, look upon us with love. In Jesus your Son you redeem us and show us the way, the truth, and the life. Grant us the freedom of your children and bring us to dwell with you always. This we ask through Christ the living Lord.
  All: Amen.

PSALM OF REJOICING
(All recite together, or alternate the verses.)
Psalm 145
Alleluia, Alleluia.
I will extol you, O my God and King,
    and I will bless your name forever and ever.
Every day will I bless you,
    and I will praise your name forever and ever.
Great is the Lord and highly to be praised;
    his greatness is unsearchable.
Generation after generation praises your works
    and proclaims your might.

Let all your works give you thanks, O Lord,
    and let your faithful ones bless you.
Let them discourse of the glory of your kingdom
    and speak of your might,
Making known to men your might
    and the glorious splendor of your kingdom.
Your kingdom is a kingdom for all ages,
    and your dominion endures through all generations.

May my mouth speak the praise of the Lord,
    and may all flesh bless his holy name
    forever and ever.
Alleluia, Alleluia.

CONCLUSION
(The leader takes the bowl of water to each person in the
group. Each person marks his or her forehead with water
in the sign of the cross saying:)
Christ has died,
Christ is risen,
Christ will come again.
Alleluia!
(If you wish, conclude with an Easter song everyone
knows.)

50

Thursdays of Easter Season

BEGINNING

(All stand. The leader lights the Easter candle.)

Leader: Christ is our light!

   All: Thanks be to God.

Leader: Let us rejoice in the Lord, our Alpha and Omega.

   All: Alleluia! Amen.

Leader: May the harvest of justice won by Christ be ours to share.

   All: May it be so for us and for all Easter people.

GATHERING

Leader: Let us call upon the God of life. (Pause a moment for silent prayer.)

Father, in the Body of Christ we live the loving Word you have spoken to the world. It is a Word of comfort and challenge, a Word which will echo until the end of time. May this holy Word resound in us and make us worthy of the name we bear, the name of Christ Jesus the Lord.

   All: Amen.

PSALM OF REJOICING

(All recite together, or alternate the verses.)

Psalm 104

Alleluia, Alleluia.

May the glory of the Lord endure forever;
   may the Lord be glad in his works!
He who looks upon the earth, and it trembles;
   who touches the mountains, and they smoke!
I will sing to the Lord all my life.
How manifold are your works, O Lord!
   In wisdom you have wrought them all—
When you send forth your spirit, they are created,
   and you renew the face of the earth.
Alleluia, Alleluia.

CONCLUSION
(The leader takes the bowl of water to each person in the group. Each person marks his or her forehead with water in the sign of the cross saying:)
Christ has died,
Christ is risen,
Christ will come again.
Alleluia!
(If you wish, conclude with an Easter song everyone knows.)

Fridays of Easter Season

BEGINNING
(All stand. The leader lights the Easter candle.)
Leader: Christ is our light!
    All: Thanks be to God.
Leader: Let us rejoice in the wholeness and holiness of the Lord.
    All: Alleluia! Amen.
Leader: May the dawn of the new age Christ has won for us light our way.
    All: May it be so for us and for all Easter people.

GATHERING
Leader: Let us call upon the God of life. (Pause for a moment of silent prayer.)
    Eternal Father, your Son has saved us in history by rising from the tomb. Transcending space and time, he frees us from death's bondage. May the presence of his Spirit among us lead us to an eternal vision of unlimited truth and unbounded love. This we ask through Christ our Lord.
    All: Amen.

PSALM OF REJOICING
(All recite together, or alternate the verses.)
Psalm 100
Alleluia, Alleluia.
Sing joyfully to the Lord, all you lands;
    serve the Lord with gladness;
    come before him with joyful song.
Know that the Lord is God;
    he made us, his we are;
    his people, the flock he tends.
Enter his gates with thanksgiving,
    his courts with praise;
Give thanks to him; bless his name, for he is good:
    the Lord, whose kindness endures forever,
    and his faithfulness, to all generations.
Alleluia, Alleluia.

CONCLUSION
(The leader takes the bowl of water to each person in the group. Each person marks his or her forehead with water in the sign of the cross saying:)
Christ has died,
Christ is risen,
Christ will come again.
Alleluia!
(If you wish, conclude with an Easter song everyone knows.)

Saturdays of Easter Season

BEGINNING
(All stand. The leader lights the Easter candle.)
Leader: Christ is our light!
    All: Thanks be to God.
Leader: Let us rejoice in the fiery presence of the living God.
    All: Alleluia! Amen.
Leader: May the victory of Christ's cross and the glory of his resurrection burn always within us.

All: May it be so for us and for all Easter people.

GATHERING

Leader: Let us call upon the God of life. (Pause a moment for silent prayer.)

Father, we thank you for your many gifts to us: for Jesus your Son, for the share we have in his death and resurrection, for this festive paschal season. Remember us always, Lord, and mark our names in your heart. This we ask through Christ our Lord.

All: Amen.

PSALM OF REJOICING

(All recite together, or alternate the verses.)

Psalm 47

Alleluia, Alleluia.

All you peoples, clap your hands,
  shout to God with cries of gladness,
For the Lord, the Most High, the awesome,
  is the great king over all the earth.
He brings peoples under us;
  nations under our feet.
He chooses for us our inheritance,
  the glory of Jacob, whom he loves.
God mounts his throne amid shouts of joy;
  the Lord, amid trumpet blasts.
Sing praise to God, sing praise;
  sing praise to our king, sing praise.
Alleluia, Alleluia.

CONCLUSION

(The leader takes the bowl of water to each person in the group. Each person marks his or her forehead with water in the sign of the cross saying:)

Christ has died,
Christ is risen,
Christ will come again.
Alleluia!

(If you wish, conclude with an Easter song everyone knows.)

THE PASCHAL LIFE

PRAYERS FOR PASCHAL PEOPLE AND PASCHAL MOMENTS

Contrary to popular opinion, the coward does not die a thousand deaths. The coward, touched by life's many demises, turns, runs, and thus dies only once—but then quite finally. Only the heroic person surrenders himself or herself to death daily, and thus finally never dies. To live this way—to continually surrender our outmoded ideas, our selfishness, and our prejudices, to struggle constantly with life's mess and meaning—this is the paschal life. But to what or to whom should we surrender ourselves? This question and the struggle to answer it have shaped the face of human endeavor throughout time.

As Christians, we surrender ourselves to Christ. We believe that Christ's is the face which has shaped all history. We believe that Christ's cross is the shape which faces us in our personal histories of dying and rising. And we believe that only a life marked by dying and rising— a paschal life—is a life worth living.

The prayers of this section are filled with the stuff of the paschal life and with the people who strive to live it. These prayers are ordinary responses to God's extraordinary presence among us. They struggle to give voice to the meaning of the Paschal Mystery in our day-to-day living, with all its surrenders, its deaths, its resurrections, and its celebrations of new life. As I said in the Introduction, these prayers do not pretend to solve the many human problems of limitations or of our relationships with ourselves, with others, and with the world around us. But they do attempt to integrate them into the paschal process, so that we might come to terms with them and ultimately surrender them into God's hands.

Finally, as with each section of this book, I hope that those who pray these prayers will come to share their personal paschal experiences with others. For only in such sharing will the Paschal Mystery come to full bloom in this life or in any other.

BRIGHT INTERVAL

Lord,
I've seen—but not clearly—
the flight of birds:
    the falcon's sudden stoop,
    the hummingbird's stand-still hover,
    the eagle's wind-riding ease,
    the sparrow's bustling flutter.
And yet none of these is flight.
Lord,
in the beat of wings—their up and down—
there is a pause, a cessation of motion;
    the wings' ascent is not eternal,
    and their descent is closed withal.
No matter the skill of the bird,
no matter the poise or majesty
of its sailing,
these motions are two,
never one.
There is always a stop
    between up and down;
always a gap in the flow
    between down and up.
These motions are two,
never one;
and the beating of wings
is but the raiment of flight.

Only in the brief halt of movement,
    in the rift between up and down and up,
only in the juncture of wings,
    unseen yet discernable
    intangible yet palpable,
there, in bright interval,
lives the magic of flight.
And you live there too, Lord,
smack-dab in the middle
of our ups and downs,
in the lacunae of living
    purposeless but meaningful
    always out of sight
    never out of touch
in the hiatus of our days.
O citizen of crises,
denizen of dreams,
you inhabit the tenuous pause
between
immanence and transcendence
between
death and rebirth.
We thank you, Lord,
for this place of your dwelling:
deep in the breach
    beyond space and time
    unreachable yet near
for there,
in bright interval,
we learn the magic of flight.
Amen.

FOR THE GIFT OF HOSPITALITY

Do not neglect to show
hospitality, for by that means
some have entertained angels
without knowing it.
HEBREWS 13:2

Open me, Lord.
Pry loose the linch-pins
  from the rusted doors
    of my time-welded apathies
    of prejudice and fear.
Favor me with your ancient gift:
    Abraham's spreading tent,
    Job's open door,
    Bethlehem's pregnant, waiting stable,
    the Merciful Father's outstretched arms,
    the festive calf fatted for the feast.
Fill me with your hospitality, Lord.
Bless me
    with insight into hearts hungry for welcome,
    with graciousness to accept the treasures they bear,
    with courage to share the gifts that are mine.
Grant, O Lord,
    that there never again may be strangers,
    only guests—sisters and brothers—
    a hosting people,
        reveling in your welcome,
        lost in your embrace.
    until we share eternal hospitality
        with you
        and the angels
        forever.
Amen.

MY MOM: A CHILD'S PRAYER

Lord,
one time Jesus' mother
asked him to do something.
And he did it quick!
I can tell Jesus loved her a lot.

I don't always do things so quick,
but I love my mom too,
and she sure does
lots of things for me.

My mom puts raisins in the oatmeal
to hide the lumps,
gives me pennies for gum machines,
and knows how to blow giant bubbles.
Sometimes my mom yells a little,
but she also sings soft songs
to make nightmares go away.

Lord,
I know most people
never call you "Mom."
But would it be okay if I did just once and awhile
'specially when I'm happy,
'specially when I'm sad?
Amen.

MY DAD: A CHILD'S PRAYER

Lord,
sometimes my dad looks silly,
especially when he wears short pants!
His legs are fuzzy.
But he doesn't care if you laugh.

My dad tells good stories
and doesn't get too angry even
when you spill two glasses
of milk at supper.

My dad hugs and tickles
and plays scarey monster.
He knows how to give rides on his back
and throw you up in the air
but never lets you fall.

Lord,
when I fail,
will you be like my dad to me?
Will you pick me up
when I fall?

My dad says you will
because you are a father
like him.
I think I will trust you, Lord,
even when it seems silly.
Amen.

TEACH US TO PRAY

Let all your works give you thanks, O Lord,
and let your faithful ones bless you.

PSALM 145

Like a bed sheet,
the water pulls itself tight
around the lake's corners,
as if daring someone to bounce
a pebble off its taut, flat surface.

Defiantly it reflects mirages
of late afternoon heat,
    slick and gleaming,
back into the fiery face
of the sun.

As the day ages, the sky whiskers over,
and a stubble of clouds
grays the sun's countenance.
The rain approaches.
An expectant breeze ripples the lake.

The birds set up a chorus
of raucous harmony
on the rain's downbeat,
and the bowl of the lake concaves
to catch each drop.

The rain comes on tiptoes at first,
then at a canter, then at a gallop;
cold and boldened, it boils in the bowl,
polishing the tarnished waters
to a silver sheen.

O Lord, we see
that even the hardest of waters
soften and wrinkle with the rain,
that even the songbirds lift their voices
to greet the summer shower.

Yet we, O Lord,
are a starched and tight-lipped people,
managing to remain well-pressed and dry
even in a downpour of your graciousness,
managing to stay close-mouthed
before a torrent of grace.

Concave us, Lord,
to catch your overflow of favor.
Ruffle our feathers
to respond to your
bountiful blessings.

For only then
can we sing with the choir of creation;
only then
will we shine
with the luster of love.
Amen.

HAUTE COUTURE

Truly you have formed my inmost being;
you knit me in my mother's womb.

PSALM 139

You are like a skillful seamstress, O God.
You separate the strands of time
and spin them into the fabric
of our lives.
With delicate patience you weave
the tapestry of our
beginning once-upon-a-times.
With intricate detail you embroider
your very presence into our
heres and nows.
With great promise you knit together
our hopes for living happily
ever after.
No moth can destroy your handiwork,
nothing rend or ravel
the threads of the seamless
stories you spin.
Therefore, we thank you
that we are so wonderfully made,
always the fashion
in season and out.
Amen.

ADOLESCENCE

O Lord,
the heavy heat buzzes
and drones like cicadas
over the sticky,
doldrum days of summer.
Even when the cutting edge
of twilight scalpels the day,
blooding the sky with ribbons
of purple and crimson flowing
into night —
even then
the spreading darkness proves
too thin-skinned to cover
and contain the pulsing
summer heat.

O Lord,
my life now seems a parade
of blazing days,
of smoldering nights,
my thick and bubbling feelings
all flowing together
into the angry cauldron
of my emotions.

O Lord,
carry me through these
hot summer days of growing;
refresh me with the soothing
breath of your Spirit;
O Lord,
help me to stay cool.
Amen.

A PRAYER FOR TEACHERS

Come, Holy Spirit,
  great infuser,
  breather of knowledge,
  windy storyteller.
Whistle your secret tunes
  to all who would share them.
Whisper your wondrous wisdom
  to those who call others to growth.
    Yes,
Come, Holy Spirit,
  answer this prayer.
We wrap it in the name of Jesus,
  the One we call Rabboni
  headmaster, teacher
  the One we call Savior,
  the One we name
Lord.
Amen.

NEW WINESKINS

Lord,
even the finest wine
   cellared too long turns vinegar,
   left to breathe too long loses its bouquet,
   opened too long goes flat.
And yet I never thought
it could happen to me.

Of course, I always prayed
to live a long life,
but never imagined
I would be forced
to grow old.
Some prayers, I surmised,
are better left unsaid.

   Or so I believed.

I say, "believed," Lord,
—past tense—
because of an extraordinary discovery:
   The joints may creak in the morning,
      but they don't crack with the day.
   The mind's wheels may turn slowly,
      but they grind exceeding fine.
   The body may seem ancient,
      but the spirit's in its prime.
   For wrinkles don't mark the ravages of time;
      they are marks of victory over time.

So, all in all, Lord,
I'm glad that I prayed them,
   those prayers for more time.
And I don't ask for new wineskins,
   only new wine.
Amen.

A SONG FOR FAITH AND FOR THOSE WHO HAVE CARRIED ITS TUNE

O clear and pristine melody,
    harmonized through the ages,
    hymned by all cultures,
    its chorus so metered,
    its grace notes surprising,
Still stir us to sing
    Holy Faith.

                                   Deo Gratias!

O song of our fathers
    and mothers,
    our sisters
    and brothers,
Most precious mellifluence,
Great rhapsody of Truth,
    Holy Faith.

                                   Deo Gratias!

O Lord, thanks are due you
    for this composition,
    your endless song.
Cascades of praise are yours too,
    O Lord,
    for the minstrels
    and singers
    who carried your tune,
    remembered the verses,
    and sang them to us
That we might teach others
    to blend in together,
    to join in the choir.
    Holy Faith.

                                   Deo Gratias!

A SHUT-IN'S PRAYER

You and I, Lord,
  we share a secret.
Sometimes it's tempting
  to give in to the sympathy,
  all those well-meant words:
    "You poor thing. You must get terribly
    lonesome."
    "You're just a living saint, my dear."
    "It's an inspiration the way you bear
    all your sufferings."
Do you see what I mean, Lord?
  It's tempting.
  But you and I share a secret.
You once said:
  "You will not enter the Kingdom
  of Heaven unless you become like
  a little child."

Well, I'm getting there, Lord.

My circle of friends and acquaintences
has dwindled considerably.
  But you, Lord, are considerate
  enough to fill the gap.
I can't even cross the street by myself.
  But take my hand, Lord,
  and I'll bear that cross.
Since I don't do anything,
I don't do anything wrong.
  But you know everything, Lord,
  so you know better!
I'm depending more and more on others.
  Thank you, Lord, more and more
  for the others who are your Church.

You and I, Lord,
   we share a secret.
   Lean down here and let me
   whisper in your ear.
Look at my loneliness, my lack of mobility,
my time-set ways, all my aches and pains.
   For whatever good they may do
   I accept and offer these "gifts"
   for the sake of those
   people who search
   for what I already possess.
Fill the beakers of their loneliness
   with the sweet fellowship
   of your Church.
Lead them by the hand on their crossing
   to faith.
Teach them that when they reach out to others,
   they touch you.
Welcome them warmly
   into the communion of saints.
Finally, grant them a share
   in your own suffering,
   and thus a portion
   in the Kingdom to come.
And me, Lord?
I'll stay right here,
   watching and waiting, praying for them,
   keeping my mouth shut,
   my heart and mind open.
And if it's all right with you, we'll just
let all this be our little secret.
   Ah, but you know me, Lord.
   I'm liable to tell everyone I know!
Amen.

FIRST STEPS

First steps are so difficult, Lord,
    and so delightful.
What agony and ecstasy
    to make and to witness.
"Come to Daddy,"
    we say,
"Come to Mommy."
And the infant defies
    his bottom-heavy gravity,
        abandons her carpet-cushioned crawl,
rises and totters into tomorrow on tiptoes.
What a risk, Lord,
    to stand up and walk!
Who else but a trusting child dares to forsake
    the four-footed security of other creatures?
Who else but a loving parent trusts to let go
    and yet holds out open arms of support?

Parent us, Lord, as we continually take
    first steps toward you.
Support us when we stumble.
Rescue us should we fall.
Plant your feet next to ours
    that we might journey together.
And walk apace with us, Lord,
    till we learn to run
    and dance to the song
piped by Christ Jesus,
    your own child.
Amen.

SAILINGMAN

Whenever I see them,
   an old man with
   a younger one,
heads bent close,
whispering the secret stories,
I feel cheated, Lord.

Whenever the wind rises sudden
on the water,
or the lake sprouts sails,
I remember my father
and rage against the loss.

Lord, my father never sailed a ship
or spent time before the mast;
but he knew how fast
a clipper would run
full-rigged before the wind.

And we never sailed together, Lord,
but only spoke of salt and foam,
and dreamed of tomorrows
cut short too quick,
too soon.

Yet my father spun
a thousand yarns
   there was a whistler in his soul
   to give his tales away
and he'd share them with me,
our heads bent close,
whispering the secret stories.

By his living
my father filled my life
with memories to hold.
By his dying
he sacrificed his tunes
for songs I had to sing.

Emptied of himself, Lord,
you were given space in him,
until the vessel of his life
spilled over
into the ocean of eternity.

I know he sails there now,
out past the sea of time,
firm at the helm at last.
And I know that you ship with him.
For, Lord,
for sure you are a sailingman
who loves a story
whistled true.
Amen.

THE PASTORAL MINISTER'S PRAYER

> . . . *when we cannot choose words in order to pray
> properly, the Spirit . . . expresses our plea in a way
> that could never be put into words.*
> ROMANS 8:26
> *The Jerusalem Bible*

I don't know what to say, Lord.
My usually facile tongue
    races ahead,
    lags behind,
    entangles itself
In the winding roads of your revelation.

What do I say to the seekers of Truth,
    Way,
    and Light?

O, you are too much for me, Lord!
   too vast and too personal,
   too profound a proclamation,
   too silent a whisper.

How may I speak the unspeakable?
How name the One who has no name?
How read between the lines
   of your brilliant, hidden face?
      Simplify, Lord.
      Simplify me.
Silence the chatter I make to entrap you.
Edit the complicated structures
   in which I've enclosed you.
Gift me with
   a newer syntax,
   a mightier metaphor,
   a more than active verb.

In the beginning was the word!

Speak that Word
   to me,
   to those I serve.
And when I don't know what to say,
   keep me quiet, Lord,
   and let your Spirit do the talking.
Amen.

FOR THE NEWLY INITIATED

Blessed are you, O Lord our God.
You give us times and seasons.
beginnings and endings,
and reasons for glad celebration.

You build up Christ's Body, the Church,
with the sinews of pilgrims,
   the blood of martyrs,
   the muscle of faith,
   and the flesh of Jesus your Son.

Look upon your daughters and sons,
our sisters and brothers, who have
   passed through the waters of life,
   received the seal of the Spirit,
   taken their place at the banquet table.
Bless them, O Lord,
with the delight of your assembly
and with the fellowship of Christ and the Spirit.

For the many treasures they bring,
we give you thanks.
For the promised years of growth and sharing ahead,
we bless your name, O Lord,
now and for endless days.
Amen.

GOLDEN BOY

"What a precious golden child!"
  whispered the great-aunt
  at his birth.
"We'll light a special candle for him."

O Lord,
he was a golden boy,
a son of Indian Summer,
  towheaded, laughing,
  rounded bright,
leaning to brilliance,
a colorful, soaring,
rainbow-winged eaglet of a child.

But as he grew, he seemed
to find the simple magic
of the heart too tame
  or the complex sorcery
  of the world too wild
to live in,
without his own peculiar conjuring,
his own forbidden alchemy.

So he came to fashion
newer, rushing wings.
And forgetting long-learned lessons,
he hit upon the tracks of a course
too deep, too steep, too close
to the devouring sun,
which melted his brief flight
and seared all the glitter,
all the color,
out of him.

He is falling fast now, Lord,
too fast for us to catch him.
Will you stretch out your saving arm,
reach out to raise him up, our precious golden child?

We'll light a special candle for him, Lord,
for his own small light
flickers and fades;
and without your cupped
and sheltering hands,
we fear the darkness
will encompass it forever.
Amen.

FOR THE NEWLY MARRIED

Lord,
bless this fresh-wed couple
with abundant riches:
with a dividend of mutual service,
with a deposit of lasting faithfulness,
with a keen interest in each other,
with a windfall of celebrating passion.

Lord,
may they be truly rich,
for they have put their riches together,
   in one another,
   in one love,
   in joint account with you.
Amen.

ON THE ANNIVERSARY OF MARRIAGE: A TOAST

Here's to the very married, Lord,
a bit thinner on top,
a tad thicker in the middle;
the years have seasoned them
and mellowed all
but their passion.

Here's to the very married, Lord.
Together they have grown,
mingling their labor and sweat,
    their joys and tears,
    their delights and their heartaches
into a full-bodied vintage
ripened with age.

Yes, here's to the very married, Lord.
As they grow old together
let them taste how you've saved them
the best wine till last;
let them quaff that sweet draught,
    heady and robust,
    as savory as time.

And here's to you too, Lord,
    the Vintner tending their vine
    and working the old miracle,
    changing water to wine.
Amen.

CRIES AND WHISPERS

Lord,
they come too soon,
those early morning cries,
too soon
to reassemble the jumble
of last evening's resolutions
of "I'll be good tomorrow."

They crack the day's foundations
before its second course is laid
and mortared in its place;
and reconstruction is so hard, Lord,
when blueprints are lost.

Still
I know somewhere amid the kitchen's cacophony
you are lurking, Lord;
somewhere between the spilt milk
and soggy cereal
salvation whispers;
in half-cups of cold coffee
your Kingdom waits
to spring its sweet surprises.

O grant me ears to hear you, Lord,
eyes to spy you in the corners
of my harried hours;
let me bear with those morning cries,
cherish those nighttime whispers,
for my redemption happens there, Lord,
or no place else
at all.
Amen.

POPSICLES: A MATTER OF DIVORCE

Lord,
I remember well as a child
the effort to break apart
the two sides of popsicles.
Too often they split,
not at their icy link,
but right across the top,
making their longed-for refreshment
difficult:
sticky to handle,
    sad to savor.
Even when the break seemed clean,
    straight down the center,
both sides came away ragged.
Wed too long,
perhaps popsicles resist
their division
with the coldest determination.
No wonder children beg
to taste them whole.

O Lord,
when our break came,
it was no clean slice,
no easy separation.
Like popsicles, the two of us
had grown so cold together—so brittle—
we seemed to resist
that inevitable division;
and when it came, it tore us
right across the top.
Our longed-for dissolution
was not as sweet,
not as refreshing,

as we had hoped
or imagined.

Still, Lord,
I know it had to be.
She and I were frozen
to each other;
and it was either the parting
or a slow and chilling death.
Now, divided,
we each make our separate,
sticky ways; both knowing
you are with us;
both hoping like children
someday
to taste you whole.
Amen.

SECRET FIRE

Lord,
my three-year-old daughter
gave me a lesson in the theology of creation.

"See, Daddy," she explained,
"firstest God takes some dust and mud
and then puts in the boney things.
Next God pushes it all in a lump
and wraps skin stuff around it."

"Oh, so that's how God makes us?"
I smiled, knowing too much,
understanding too little.

She shook her curly head.
"Unh, uh," she pouted, hands on hips,
a look of pity in her eyes.
"Nextest, God puts the lump
in secret fire,
and then we come alive!"

Lord,
hours of reading,
months of lectures,
years of study,
two decades of schooling,
have not given me such insight,
have not afforded me such vision.

O Lord,
that I could see you
through my daughter's eyes,
catch but a glimpse
of your creative passion,
and experience again
your secret fire!
Amen.

PASCHAL PEOPLE

Lord,
we are a people
heavy with experience
   of darkness and light
   of water and fire
   of passion and compassion
   of dying and rebirth
all paschal people, Lord,
ripe with the meaning
of you.
Amen.

APPENDIX

USING BRIGHT INTERVALS
WITH AND FOR CATECHUMENS

The Introduction to the *Rite of Christian Initiation of Adults* speaks of the potential for parish renewal in the rites of Christian initiation.[4] By reestablishing initiation as the pivotal public event of the life of the Church, the RCIA offers the paschal experience of initiation (i.e., conversion, transformation, death and resurrection) not only to adult candidates (catechumens), but also to the parish community which welcomes and initiates them. In other words, the RCIA provides a locus for individual and communal paschal experience as well as the arena in which the Church enters most fully into the Paschal Mystery of Christ. From a pastoral standpoint, however, the presence of a few catechumens in its midst touches a large parish community only minimally. And although many ministries, such as those of catechist and sponsor, have developed around the catechumenate, these ministries also touch only a few. So the community of believers still faces the question of how to renew itself through the initiation of new members.

One way, and only one, is by calling the faith community to prayer. Traditionally, the Church accomplishes this through its rituals of worship. Hence the revised *rites* of initiation.

Still, if a parish wants the rites of initiation to be powerful and meaningful community events, those rituals must flow from a community vitalized by personal and shared prayer. Power and meaning cannot and will not arise simply from revitalized rituals. The following outline addresses this pastoral need. It lists suggestions for using the contents of *Bright Intervals* to provide opportunities for members of the faith community to support the catechumens in their midst and to renew their own faith as they journey in prayer with the catechumens to the great feast of Easter.

Prayers to Support the Rituals of Catechumenate

Daily Prayer with and for the Catechumens

(Parishioners may use these prayers individually, with their families, or in larger prayer groups. Including the catechumens in such prayer groups not only helps to initiate the catechumens into the paschal life; it also gives the parish community an opportunity to come to know the catechumens more deeply and to offer them personal and prayerful support and witness. When such sharing takes place, catechumens and faithful join one another on the paschal journey.)

Prayers for Catechists and Sponsors

Individual Prayers for the Catechumens

In its statement "The Parish: A People, A Mission, A Structure," the National Conference of Catholic Bishops urges parishes and parishioners to "acknowledge the identity they have in common and demonstrate the responsibility they have for one another."[5] I believe that *Bright Intervals,* used in the manner outlined above, can help parishes accomplish this important mission. Since prayer, whether private or shared, is a response to God's loving initiative, and since private and communal prayer lead to and underpin liturgical celebration, a parish's use of *Bright Intervals* to support the conversion journey of its catechumens can help all the parishioners to a greater share in the ministry of sacramental initiation which truly belongs to them. I believe that using this book can also "help the catechumens to grasp the full breadth of God's call to . . . the commitment of baptism [which] is to join with the church community in an unending effort to deepen its relationship with God."[6]

May the paschal prayer and experiences you share lead you to a profound fellowship with God and with one another. May your active concern for one another foster a deeper commitment to the paschal life. And, finally, may all life's intervals be bright.

NOTES

1. Fyodor Dostoevsky, *The Brothers Karamazov,* trans. Constance Garnett (New York: Modern Library, 1958).

2. T.S. Eliot, "Little Gidding" from *Four Quartets,* in *The Norton Anthology of English Literature,* ed. M.H. Abrams (New York: W.W. Norton & Company, Inc., 1968), II, p. 2197.

3. G.K. Chesterton, "The House of Christmas," in *The Collected Poems of G.K. Chesterton,* introduction by Daniel B. Dodson (New York: Dodd, Mead & Company, 1980).

4. Number 4: "The initiation of catechumens takes place step by step in the midst of the community of the faithful. Together with the catechumens, the faithful reflect upon the value of the paschal mystery [and] renew their own conversion. . . ." Number 41: ". . . the people of God, represented by the local church, should always understand and show that the initiation of adults [catechumens] is its concern and the business of all the baptized." From *The Rites of the Catholic Church* as Revised by the Second Vatican Council (New York: Pueblo Publishing Company, 1976), pp. 20 and 31.

5. National Conference of Catholic Bishops, *The Parish: A People, A Mission, A Structure* (Washington, D. C.: United States Catholic Conference Publications Office, 1980), p. 10.

6. Ibid., p. 9.